MW01223114

# when
# I look into
## the
# sea

Cheryl Woodruff Brooks

Illustrated by Neha Anwar

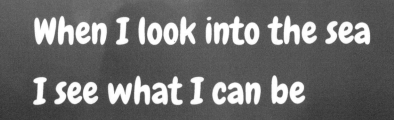

When I look into the sea
I see what I can be

I see my dreams before my eyes
I look with wonder and surprise

Because I believe in me
When I look into the sea

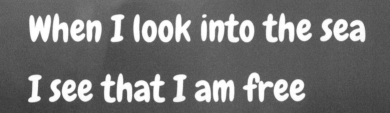

When I look into the sea
I see that I am free

I know that I can soar
From the sky and to the ocean floor

Because I believe in me
When I look into the sea

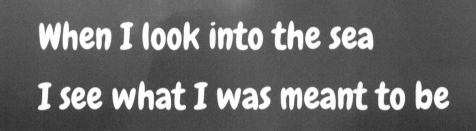

When I look into the sea
I see what I was meant to be

I will grow and learn each day
While I still make time to play

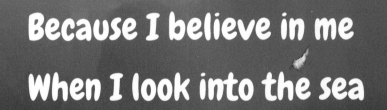

Because I believe in me
When I look into the sea

CPSIA information can be obtained
at www.ICGtesting.com
Printed in the USA
BVHW010758200123
656658BV00004B/9